AF413178

THE SNOWMAN'S GOT FROSTBITE!

WINTER AROUND THE WORLD

NATURE BOOKS FOR BEGINNERS

Children's Nature Books

Speedy Publishing LLC
40 E. Main St. #1156
Newark, DE 19711
www.speedypublishing.com

Winter is the colder season, when you have to put on lots of clothes to go outside. Read on and find out what the weather can do, and what people do to celebrate winter.

Snowmen Family.

WINTER CAN BE CHILLY

Outside of the tropics, the daily temperature gets lower in the winter. Lots of plants and some animals hibernate, slowing their systems down and basically sleep their way through the cold months. Rivers and lakes can freeze, and huge drifts of snow can pile up.

IT CAN SNOW ALMOST ANYWHERE

The Atacama Desert in Chili gets almost no rainfall at all most years, and certainly no snow. But because of a mass of cold air moving up from Antarctica in 2011, over 30 inches of snow fell on the desert in a single storm.

Father with kids running in beautiful winter forest.

SNOW IS FLUFFY

Rain is drops of water, often wrapped around a fragment of dust or other material. Snow includes a lot of air, so it is like whipped-up water. The same precipitation that would make one inch of rain in warm weather can make about ten inches of snow in the winter.

Natural snowflakes on snow.

THE TEMPERATURE CAN DROP SUDDENLY

Even if the winter day is mild, you should take a jacket with you when you go out. A change in weather conditions can send the temperature falling very quickly and dangerously. In 1911 in Rapid City, South Dakota one winter day, the temperature dropped in 15 minutes from 55 down to 8 degrees Fahrenheit.

THE SNOWIEST CITY

In northern Japan, Aomori City averages over 25 feet of snow every winter.

Shirakawago Covered in Snow.

CELEBRATING WINTER

Around the world, people and societies have developed ways of putting some enjoyment into winter. They celebrate the end of the old year and the start of the new one, the day when daylight hours start getting longer again, and religious events like Christmas.

CHRISTMAS

For many in today's world, Christmas is about the presents you get, but the spirit of Christmas is more connected with the gifts you give to others. The gift-giving is a small part of the festivities to mark the birth of Jesus Christ. In the Bible there is a story of Wise Men who travel a long distance to find the baby Jesus. When they find him they give him gifts to honor him as the Son of God.

Kids decorating Christmas tree in beautiful living room.

KRAMPUS

Around Christmas time in Austria, people dress up as devils and tell stories of how Krampus will come and punish naughty children. In the stories, Krampus carries very bad children away in a sack!

LOSAR

In Tibet, the New Year (Losar) celebration lasts fifteen days. There are special things to drink and eat, and special clothing to wear and dances to perform. On the last day of the festival everyone cleans houses and public buildings, and makes ready to welcome the new year.

EID AL ADHA

The Muslim Festival of the Sacrifice happens from the tenth to the thirteenth day of the twelfth lunar month. It marks when Abraham was willing to sacrifice Isaac, his own son (in the end, he didn't have to!). Those who can afford it, sacrifice an animal to make a feast. The meat is divided into three parts: one part for family, one part for friends, and one part for people in need.

Tibetian Prayer Flags - Every year during Losar (New Year) the flags are changed for new and freshly colored ones.

LA QUEMA DEL DIABLO

The Burning of the Devil takes place in Guatemala on December 7. People burn statues of the devil in the town square, as a sign of getting rid of the bad things of the past year.

CHRISTMAS BONFIRES

The people of New Orleans, Louisiana, build high bonfires along the levees, the high, artificial banks of the Mississippi River. Some bonfires are even built to look like castles or river boats. They light the bonfires on Christmas Eve.

THE YULE LADS

In Iceland, the Yule Lads are 13 creatures who bring gifts to children in the 13 nights leading up to Christmas. Children put a shoe on the windowsill and, if they've been good, that night's Yule Lad will leave a small gift there. If they have not been good, they may find a rotten potato in their shoe in the morning!

Beautiful winter morning in the mountains.

MARI LWYD

In Wales around Christmas time, groups go from house to house, singing traditional songs and carrying the skull of a horse (Mari Lwyd, or The Grey Mare). They sing for the family in each house, and the family invites the singers (and the horse!) into the house for refreshments.

WINTER CARNIVAL

In Quebec City in Canada, and in many other northern cities around the world, people hold an annual winter carnival. The event spans many days, and includes fireworks, races on skis or skates, or with dog teams, and competitions to build ice sculptures. People turn out despite the cold to enjoy making a few bright days in the dark of winter.

BELSNICKEL

Belsnickel is a scary character from German legends. People as far away as Newfoundland and Pennsylvania keep up the Belsnickel tradition. In Newfoundland, for instance, *"Belsnickel"* and his followers pretend to invade homes on New Year's Day, bringing singing, dancing, and jokes. The householders have to provide food and drink for the Belsnickelers. Belsnickel is one of many traditions of a winter character who is sort of the opposite of Santa Claus.

Annaberg-Buchholz christmas.

Winter wonderland with mountain chalets in the Alps.

KIVIAK

The Inuit of Greenland have a traditional winter food called kiviak. They take a seal carcass and hollow it out. Into the carcass they put hundreds of small birds, with their feathers and feet and everything, and with the birds they add seal fat. The Inuit press the air out of the seal skin, and then seal the opening with more fat.

They then bury the carcass under rocks for months, or even a year. The birds ferment inside the skin and are ready to eat in the part of the winter when there are not many birds to hunt... and people are hungry enough to want to eat them!

HIDE THE BROOMS!

In Norway, people hide their brooms on Christmas Eve. This is so witches and other evil spirits can't find the brooms and ride around on them.

THE NIGHT OF THE RADISHES

In Oaxaca in Mexico, there is a three-day festival just before Christmas called The Night of the Radishes. People carve vegetables, especially radishes, into figures to make scenes from folk stories, and from the Bible.

Christmas tree in front of the Norwegian Parliament.

Professio

POLAR BEAR SWIM

In January across North America, people gather for a charity event called the Polar Bear Swim. Participants contribute to charity to have the right to jump into the cold winter waters of a lake or the ocean where the event is held. Participants have to wear regular bathing suits, not divers' wet suits, but some also wear funny hats.

Polar/Ice Plunge event at the 2016 Ullrfest winter festival.

Family celebrating Christmas.

CEMETERY VISIT

In Finland, many families spend part of Christmas Eve or the evening of Christmas day visiting the graves of ancestors and other loved ones. They leave candles burning at the gravesides, so cemeteries sparkle with tiny lights in the dark winter night.

Cemetery lit up by candle light.

YALDA NIGHT

In Iran, Yalda Night is the winter solstice, the shortest day of the year. *"Yalda"* means *"Birth",* so the festival marks the birth of the new year. Families stay up all night together, talking, singing, and eating special foods.

Yalda Night table in the celebration of Persians (Iranians).

THE MARRIAGE SHOE

In the Czech Republic, single women have a funny tradition. On Christmas Day they go outside and throw a shoe at their house, to see if they will get married in the coming year. If the shoe lands with its heel closest to the house, then the answer is no: no marriage this year!

Christmas In Prague.

DONG ZHI

In China and Southeast Asia, people celebrate the arrival of winter with the Dong Zhi celebration around December 22. People eat special rice dumplings called tangyuan, and worship their ancestors.

Sweet tangyuan glutinous rice dessert eaten in China and Taiwan.

SOYAL

Soyal is the winter solstice celebration of the Hopi Indians in Arizona. On the shortest day of the year, the Hopi people hold dances, cleansing ceremonies, feasts, and other events to welcome the Kachinas. The Kachinas are good spirits that live in the mountains, and the Hopi ask them to protect the people in the coming year.

Hopi Indians performing a Snake Dance at Pueblo of Oraibi, Arizona, ca.1896

Roman
Tg. Neamţ
Bacău
CENTER
FORUM SHOPPING

URSUL

The Bear Dance, or Ursul, takes place in Romania on New Year's Eve. People dress up as bears and dance, and in some way this is supposed to make sure the harvest will be good in the new year. In the past, people kept real bears and forced them to dance for this celebration, but now it is all people in costumes.

Bear costume parade.

SAINT LUCIA DAY

In Sweden, on Saint Lucia Day (December 13), the youngest girl in each family dresses up as Saint Lucy of Syracuse (in Italy). She was an early Christian martyr. The girl wears a white dress with a red sash, and a crown of greenery and candles. The girl leads the family outside where they join with other families for food and singing.

Saint Lucy's Day.

Advent Candles on Christmas Eve - representing
Prophecy, Love, Joy, Peace and Purity.

A MERRY WINTER

How do you celebrate the winter? What are the customs in your town? Make sure you take part in them when the weather gets cold!

Read more Baby Professor books, like *No Kidding! Interesting Facts about April Fool's Day* and *The Chinese Festivals,* to learn more about celebrations and traditions around the world.

Visit
BABY PROFESSOR
EDUCATION KIDS
www.BabyProfessorBooks.com
to download Free Baby Professor eBooks
and view our catalog of new and exciting
Children's Books